# COILS, MAGNETS AND RINGS

## MICHAEL FARADAY'S WORLD

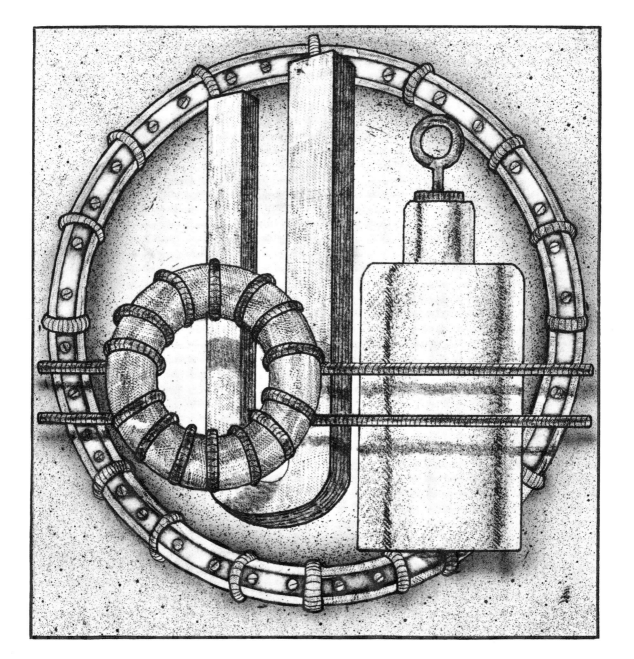

# COILS, MAGNETS AND RINGS

## MICHAEL FARADAY'S WORLD

by Nancy Veglahn
illustrated by Christopher Spollen

Coward, McCann & Geoghegan, Inc.    New York

For Dan and Ruth

Text copyright © 1976 by Nancy Veglahn
Illustrations copyright © 1976 by Christopher Spollen

SBN: TR-698-20384-4  SBN: GB-698-30636-8

LIBRARY OF CONGRESS CATALOGING IN PUBLICATION DATA
Veglahn, Nancy. Coils, magnets, and rings.
Summary: A biography of the English scientist who believed
that one should never stop asking questions. His questions
led him to discoveries concerning electricity.
1. Faraday, Michael, 1791–1867—Juvenile literature.
[1. Faraday, Michael, 1791–1867. 2. Scientists]
I. Spollen, Christopher J. II. Title.
QC16.F2V43  530′.092′4 (B) (92)  76-14385
Printed in the United States of America

# Contents

# Contents

# 1
# The Blacksmith's Boy

Michael Faraday was always asking questions.

He asked so many questions because he wondered about everything. He wondered what makes people sneeze, and whether flies have bones, and why candles burn, and what keeps the stars in order. It was not easy to get answers to questions like these in Michael Faraday's part of London at the beginning of the nineteenth century. But he kept asking and wondering.

When his father heated the blacksmith's forge, Michael wondered why the iron horseshoe nails became soft when they were heated, but the anvil didn't. When his mother baked bread, he wondered how the little bit of yeast she put in the dough could make the whole loaf rise. When his baby sister, Margaret, learned to walk, he wondered how she did it, and that made him wonder how *he* could walk, until he stumbled over his own feet trying to figure it out.

Most of all, Michael wondered why nobody else seemed to

wonder as he did. His friends played marbles with him on the street, then went home shrugging their shoulders when he started asking his questions. His parents were too busy wondering how to get enough money to feed their four children and pay the bills to even try to answer. His teacher told him to practice his numbers.

Soon Michael could not ask his questions at school because he had to get a job. His father got sick and could no longer earn much money as a blacksmith. Michael's older brother, Robert, went to work first. Then, when he was ten years old, Michael stopped going to school and became an errand boy.

He worked for a bookbinder, Mr. Riebau. In Riebau's shop, the pages of new books were sewn together in order and the covers glued on. Old, worn books were fixed and given new covers. Mr. Riebau also loaned newspapers to a list of customers. In those days, most people could not afford to buy newspapers. They paid a small sum to borrow them.

Michael's job was to take the papers from house to house. He waited while one customer read the paper before taking it on to the next. Michael did not feel this job was boring because it gave him a chance to think. One day he was waiting on a customer's front step when he noticed an iron railing beside the door. Having nothing better to do, he stuck his head through it.

"Which side of this railing am I really on?" he wondered. "I

do all my thinking and seeing with my head, so it seems like I'm on the side where my head is. But most of my body is on the *other* side."

He went on wondering about that until the door opened and knocked him against the railing. His nose started to bleed. As he took the paper on to the next customer, he thought about that. What makes a wound stop bleeding? What is blood? Why do people die if they bleed too much? And so on.

Delivering his newspapers, Michael walked all over London. More than a million people lived there in 1802. Many of them, like Michael's father, had recently come to the city from country towns. The streets were crowded with people and carts and wagons and carriages. Sometimes a flock of sheep stopped traffic. Shops along the streets sold goods from all over the world. Colorful signs swung above the shop doors, advertising: "Shoes Mended Here;" "Children Educated Here;" "R. Bixby, Hatter;" or "Rolling Pins."

Most of the homes and shops in London were heated by coal fires. That made the air very smoky. Even the cabbages and radishes in London tasted of smoke. Sometimes Michael had trouble finding his way, especially if it was raining or foggy. He had to watch carefully to avoid being knocked down by the wagons and carriages or being hit by garbage. People often threw their garbage out the window and onto the street!

Still, Michael thought about his questions even when there

was no one to ask and he was in a hurry. Why were there so many people in London? Was there a way to heat the buildings with something besides coal so the air would be clear as in the country? What made lightning?

When he got back to Mr. Riebau's shop, Michael also had to sweep the floors, wash the windows, and keep things tidy. He liked working in the bookbinder's shop. He liked the smells of ink and glue and leather and crisp new paper. He liked Mr. Riebau. Most of all, he liked to read.

When he had time, Michael read the newspapers he delivered. Stories of wars and revolutions, new governments and old governments, courts and laws all marched across the pages of the newspapers like tiny armies of black type. Sometimes Michael found articles about new inventions and scientific discoveries. He read these very carefully and thought about the people who figure out how things work.

Several older boys worked in Mr. Riebau's shop and lived in his house. They were called apprentices. These boys would work for the bookbinder for seven years; then they had learned enough to become bookbinders themselves. Michael watched them helping Mr. Riebau put new covers on worn-out books. Of course, he asked a lot of questions.

One day when Michael was fourteen years old, Mr. Riebau asked *him* a question. "You seem to like watching us work. Wouldn't you like to move here and be an apprentice?"

# 2
# The Bookbinder's Apprentice

Michael Faraday lived and worked at Mr. Riebau's shop for seven years. He learned all the skills of a bookbinder: how to assemble the pages of a book in the right order, how to sew them and pound them together with a wooden mallet so they would lie flat, how to cut the leather for the covers, and how to glue the finished books together.

The shop was a pleasant work place. Mr. Riebau let his apprentices talk and joke while they assembled and repaired books. Often he joined in the fun. And he let Michael read before work, after work, at mealtime—whenever there was a spare moment. At first, Michael was sure the answers to all his questions were in those books. He read everything that was sent to Mr. Riebau for binding: *Arabian Nights*, the plays of Shakespeare, a book of sermons, a history of England, nursery rhymes, scientific studies.

The trouble was that instead of answering his questions, the books often brought up new ones. And he was afraid he might forget the answers he did find. So he started a notebook. By now, Michael knew enough about bookbinding to make his own notebook from scraps in the shop. Carefully, he wrote down all the bits of information that he wanted to remember. He even made an index, so that he could find each note on "Fairy Rings" and "Flies" and "Legends" and "Balloons."

Then one day, Michael had the chance to read the "E" volume of the *Encyclopedia Britannica*. There was not time to read all of it, of course. The book would only be in Mr. Riebau's shop for a few days. He had to skip over sections like "Egg" and "Egret" and "Elamite."

But when he came to the article on "Electricity," Michael read every word. That took him several hours, because it was 127 pages long. He copied much of the information into his notebook. Electricity was one of the things Michael had wondered most about. Newspaper articles about scientific subjects spoke of electricity as a sort of curious force in nature that no one understood.

The word "electric," Michael learned, comes from the Greek word for amber, a kind of rock. Long ago, the Greeks had noticed that if they rubbed a piece of amber with a soft cloth, the cloth would attract bits of plants or feathers. Other ancient people had discovered rocks they called "lodestones" which attracted scraps of metal. These lodestones, which actually

contained a certain kind of iron ore now called magnetite, were found in the ancient country of Magnesia, and so the lodestones came to be known as magnets.

Many years later, people learned that one end of a magnet or a piece of lodestone was attracted to the earth's North Pole, and the other end to the South Pole. So people called the end that pointed north the magnet's North Pole; the other end became known as the South Pole of the magnet. Sailors used magnets to make compasses which helped them steer their ships on long journeys; the magnetic needle of the compass always pointed in the direction of north.

This put the power of magnetism to work. But no one really understood how or why it worked. Some people thought that the forces of electricity and magnetism were similar. Both did have the power to attract objects over a distance. But how did they work? How were they alike? Was there a connection between magnetism and electricity?

Michael read of an American named Benjamin Franklin who had thought of an interesting way to prove that lightning and electricity were the same thing. Almost fifty years earlier, Dr. Franklin had fastened a key to one end of a long wire and a kite to the other. By flying his kite in a thunderstorm, Dr. Franklin had shown that an electrical charge was produced by the lightning and traveled down the wire to the key. Michael wished that he could have met this American who was curious enough to fly a kite in the rain.

He read of another invention called a "Leyden jar." This device was simply a glass jar with a cork in the opening. Half the inside and half the outside of the jar was coated with a thin metal (like our tinfoil) and then a brass rod was put through the cork. The jar could be used to store up an electric charge and save it, almost as Michael's mother saved dried beans or tea in her glass jars.

A French scientist had used a Leyden jar to show that electricity could pass through people's bodies. He had lined up seven hundred monks in a Paris monastery and told them to hold hands. When the first monk got a shock from the Leyden jar, all seven hundred men jumped!

Still, no one knew what caused electricity or how it worked.

"I could make a Leyden jar," Michael thought. He liked reading articles like the one on electricity, but they never had enough answers for him. Now he wondered whether he might be able to find his own answers. The trouble was, he had no money. Most of the small amount he earned was needed at home. It seemed silly to think of setting up a scientific laboratory when he had holes in his shoes.

But Michael did not give up easily. One day, he noticed two glass jars in the window of a secondhand store on Little Chesterfield Street. They were just right for Leyden jars—but he didn't have even the small sum needed to buy them. He waited.

The jars got dusty, and after awhile the store owner reduced the price. Still they didn't sell, and Michael waited. Early each morning when he went out for a walk before work, he looked in the cluttered window to see the price marked on the jars. Finally, when they cost only a few pennies, he bought them.

Mr. Riebau let Michael have scraps of metal, wood, and glass, and bits of glue left over from bookbinding. He also agreed to let Michael use the back of the shop at night for his scientific experiments.

When Michael finished the Leyden jar, he called the other apprentices in to show it to them. They jumped back when he touched the brass rod and made it spark.

"But what's it *for?*" they asked.

"I can store electricity in it."

"Why?"

Michael had no answer for that, and they went off to bed, smiling and shaking their heads.

The shop was quiet at night. It was a good time to work and think. Michael built up the fire in the fireplace and used it to heat chemicals and melt metals. He set up his experiments along the mantelpiece. Shadows danced on the walls and ceil-

ing as he worked. Sometimes one of his concoctions went wrong and exploded with a "pop." Usually by the time he dragged himself up the stairs to bed he had learned something, even if it was only what *not* to try again.

One day Mr. Riebau was talking to a wealthy customer, a Mr. Dance, about some new scientific books. "I have a boy here who'll want to read those," Mr. Riebau said, and told Mr. Dance about his curious apprentice. He called Michael into the room and had him show the man his notebook and his Leyden jar.

"Have you ever gone to hear the scientific lectures at the Royal Institution?" Mr. Dance asked.

Michael shook his head.

"A boy with your interests shouldn't miss those. Sir Humphry Davy is speaking in a few weeks."

Michael had no answer. He knew that Sir Humphry Davy was the greatest scientist in England, and that the Royal Institution was the place where Davy and many other scientists did their work. He also knew that the lectures cost money.

Mr. Dance must have understood Michael's problem, because a few days later he came back to the bookbinder's shop with tickets to four lectures by Sir Humphry Davy.

# 3
# The Royal Institution

It was February, 1812. Napoleon's armies had conquered most of Europe. British soldiers were fighting the French in Spain and the Americans across the Atlantic. King George III, ruler of England, had lost his mind, and others had to run the government. Michael Faraday knew all this, but he thought of nothing but the lectures. He saved scraps of paper Mr. Riebau didn't need, and washed out his best clothes, and trimmed his hair.

On the night of the first lecture he walked through lightly falling snow to Number 21 Albemarle Street. The Royal Institution was a large building of gray stone with fourteen pillars across the front. It looked as wonderful as a castle from the *Arabian Nights*, and as Michael walked up the wide stairs inside he felt sure there were amazing secrets hidden behind each closed door.

He found a seat in the crowded lecture hall, and soon Sir Humphry Davy appeared on the platform. As the great man

spoke, Michael wrote down everything. His fingers ached, his eyes burned from writing in the dimly lit room. He had no time to think about all the facts and theories Davy talked about. He would do that later.

In the next few weeks Michael copied the notes into a fresh notebook he had made. He drew pictures to show the equipment Davy had used on the platform and the experiments he had done. There was another lecture in March and two in April. Michael took careful notes on all of them.

The finished notebook with its pictures was 386 pages long! It was full of facts about chemicals and gases and steam engines and the laws of nature.

But still—Michael had questions. He had more questions than ever.

His years as Mr. Riebau's apprentice were almost over. In a few months he would be ready to go to work as a "journey-man" bookbinder, and some day perhaps he would have his own shop. It was a good trade, and he liked it. Yet he could not forget the Royal Institution.

Faraday had a daring idea. Why not ask Sir Humphry Davy whether there might be work for him at the Institution? Why not send him those lecture notes to show him that Michael Faraday could listen and learn? He put the notes in a neat package, included a letter, and sent the bundle to Sir Humphry Davy.

Months crawled by with no answer. Michael began to lose hope for the first time. He was twenty-two years old, a grown man with no money and no education except what he had found for himself. Maybe it was silly to dream of becoming a scientist. There was nothing wrong with working as a bookbinder.

One night early in 1813, Michael was getting ready for bed when he heard someone knocking loudly at the door. He looked out the window and saw a fancy carriage in the street. When he opened the door, he was even more startled to see a footman in a powdered wig and a coat with bright brass buttons. The man handed him a note. Michael was too surprised to say anything, and the footman got back into the carriage and drove away. Using a coal from the fire, Michael lit a candle and looked at the note. It was addressed to him.

Sir Humphry Davy wanted Michael Faraday to call the next morning at the Royal Institution.

After a sleepless night, Michael put on his best suit and walked to the big stone building in Albemarle Street. A doorman directed him to the office of Sir Humphry Davy.

"I had to fire one of our laboratory assistants yesterday," Davy told him. "Got into a fight—the man was a troublemaker from the beginning. I need a helper to keep my equipment in order and write up the records and perhaps even help me prepare for experiments. I remembered your letter, and those amazing notes you took on my lectures. . . ."

The salary would be a guinea a week, plus fuel, candles, and aprons. Best of all, Michael could live in the Royal Institution; there was a room available on the top floor. Michael made a bundle of his few extra clothes, his notebook and other belongings. He left his homemade laboratory equipment behind; he would have better things to work with at the Royal Institution. A charwoman showed him to his room that evening. The roof slanted over his head, and the windows were small and dusty. All the furniture he needed was there: a narrow bed, a desk, some wooden chairs.

In the middle of the night Michael was still awake, his heart thudding with excitement. He got up and lit a candle. Then he pulled his clothes on and crept down the stairs, through the wide hall and into the laboratory where he was to work with Sir Humphry Davy.

Sir Humphry had shown the room to him earlier, but it looked different at night. The faint candleglow showed hints of the wonders of that room: gleaming glass jars and bright metal tools and mysterious chemicals stored on shelves that reached from floor to ceiling. A mixture of powerful smells made Michael's nose twitch. He would have to get used to all those chemical odors; they were even stronger than the smells

of the bookbinding shop. A bit of hot wax stung his thumb. He looked down at the candle and wondered suddenly how it worked. He had been using candles all his life, but he had never noticed before that the flame was brighter at the top and bottom than in the middle. Why was that? He went back upstairs, climbed into bed, and fell asleep, thinking about candles.

He started work in the wonderful laboratory the next morning. At first he only washed and dried the equipment and learned where everything was. But soon Sir Humphry let him help with the experiments themselves, and Michael began to feel like a scientist at last.

There were a few problems. Sometimes the experiments did not go just as Sir Humphry planned. That was what made them *experiments!* In his first weeks at the Institution, Michael helped Sir Humphry work with the chemical nitrogen trichloride. The first batch Michael mixed blew up and ripped his hand open. The next morning he tried again, and the explosion cut his eyelid and ruined some equipment. The third time, Sir Humphry was there. The famous scientist received a cut on the face and a blow to the head. After the fourth explosion they gave up.

Then there was Mrs. Davy. Michael did not see much of her until he was invited to go along with the Davy's on a trip

through Europe. The trouble began before they got on the boat at Plymouth.

"You," she said sharply to Michael, "get my bags out of the carriage."

Michael stood amid his own belongings. He thought that she was talking to someone else—a porter or a servant.

"I said, get my bags!" she commanded. Sir Humphry looked embarrassed. He explained that his valet had refused to come on the trip. Davy was sure Michael wouldn't mind lending a hand. . . .

So the blacksmith's son traveled to France, Italy, and Switzerland with Sir Humphry Davy and his wife. Michael met great scientists in many cities and listened as they discussed their work. But he also had to run errands and carry packages and post letters. Worst of all, he had to try to be polite to Mrs. Davy, who treated him like a servant and would not even let him eat at the table with the family and their guests.

She talked all the time. Once a sudden storm came up when they were on a boat in the Gulf of Genoa. The storm was a great relief to Michael, although it almost sank the boat. Mrs. Davy nearly fainted; she was so frightened that she stopped talking at last.

Michael Faraday promised himself that he would never, never, *never* get married. In the end, he was glad to get home to London.

Soon after the trip, Faraday was given a new, fancy title. He had done so well as Davy's assistant that he was promoted to "Assistant and Superintendent of the Apparatus of the Laboratory and Mineralogical Collection." This long title meant that he could now do some of his own experiments as well as helping the senior scientists.

He was too busy to leave the Royal Institution very often. Sometimes he went out for dinner with friends or to the theater. On Sundays he attended church. Faraday belonged to a very small religious group called the Sandemanians.

It was at church that he met Sarah Barnard. She was a quiet, dark-haired girl with a merry smile. Sometimes they talked after the services were over. He liked talking with her so much that he missed her when her family was away from London. So he began writing letters to her. He even thought about what a good wife she would be. And then he remembered Mrs. Davy. No! He would never get married. He spent more and more hours in the laboratory and tried to forget "Sally."

But he couldn't do it. Finally one day Mrs. Davy came to the laboratory to scold her husband about something, and Faraday stood listening to her harsh and endless talk. Sally Barnard was nothing like Mrs. Davy! And she never would be.

The next time he saw her, Michael asked Sally to marry him.

The young couple moved into a larger apartment in the

Royal Institution. Sally immediately made friends of all the people there, from the charwomen to the top scientists. She gave parties and had relatives come to visit and fixed the apartment into a sort of home. Faraday would climb the stairs to their rooms after hours of experimenting to find the apartment warmed by a bright fire and full of the smell of good food. He forgot the laboratory and the unanswered questions of the day, and for a few hours he was simply happy. He needed that change of pace every evening, because his work took most of his energy. It was an exciting time to be a scientist. All over the world, discoveries were being made about the laws of nature. Each new discovery led to more experiments and more discoveries.

# 4
# "There It Goes!"

One morning in 1820, Sir Humphry Davy rushed into the laboratory with a handful of papers.

"Faraday, listen to this! It's been proven—there is a connection between electricity and magnetism! I just got the report from Denmark."

Michael put down the chemicals he was mixing and listened as Sir Humphry told him about the new discovery. A Danish scientist named Hans Oersted had found that an electrical current could change the direction of a compass needle.

Faraday and Davy pushed everything else aside to try the Dane's experiment. They found a compass and covered it with a piece of glass. Then they ran a thin wire over the glass and connected it to a battery. They watched as the electric current from the battery went through the wire. And it worked! The needle of the compass moved!

In the following months, Faraday kept coming back to the experiment and doing it again in different ways. Sometimes the compass needle seemed to be pulled toward the charged wire, and sometimes it appeared to be pushed away. Faraday wanted to know why.

Late one fall afternoon, Faraday sat studying the journal he kept in the laboratory. Everyone else had gone, and he knew that Sally would have his supper ready upstairs. But something about the numbers and drawings in his journal bothered him. He had drawn little arrows to show the direction in which the compass needle had moved at different times when he tried Oersted's experiment. He stared at the page until the arrows began to swim before his eyes like minnows in a pond. Push-pull, push-pull. What was the secret?

Faraday wondered what would happen if the wire carrying electricity were free to *move* above a magnet. The magnet would have to be powerful. . . . He looked up from his journal to the tall shelves against the wall. A bar magnet would pull at the wire with much more force than the compass. And the pull would be the greatest at the end, or pole, of the magnet.

He got a bar magnet from the shelf and stuck it into a blob of wax, so that one pole pointed up. Still he was not satisfied with the arrangement. The pole was too small to make the wire move very much. Faraday took a deep bowl and put the wax in the bottom of it. He stuck the magnet in the wax again and then filled the bowl almost to the top with mercury. Because mercury is a liquid metal, he knew that the magnet would make the mercury magnetic too.

George Barnard, Faraday's brother-in-law, often stopped in to eat with them. He stuck his head through the doorway now and said, "Supper's getting cold. Sally wants to know when you'll be up."

"George! Come in. Help me fix this. It shouldn't take long."

While they rigged an electric circuit above the magnet in its bowl of mercury, Faraday explained his idea. If the "push" and the "pull" were exactly the same, it seemed to him that the wire would go around in a circle. They would soon know whether he was right or wrong.

At last they had the wire suspended above the pole of the magnet, and Faraday connected the circuit to a battery to send a current of electricity through the wire.

"There it goes! There it goes!" he shouted as the wire began to move around his magnet in a perfect circle. Watching it, Faraday was so delighted that he danced around the table, laughing and slapping George on the shoulder.

When he had calmed down enough to write a complete description of the experiment in his journal, Michael glanced at the clock near the door. "Can it be that late?"

"Sally sent me to get you more than an hour ago."

"We'll go out to eat—and to the theater! We should celebrate. I think I've learned something new."

Faraday had learned that the power of a magnet will make an electrically charged wire move around its pole in a circle. He had no idea then how important his findings would be. They made it possible for inventors working years later to build the first electric motors. But at the time, Faraday's discovery was just an interesting piece of information. No one knew quite what to do with it, because no one understood enough about the mysterious power called electricity.

Faraday kept coming back to it in the following years. His notebooks bulged with accounts of experiments using magnets, wires, and batteries. Most of these experiments didn't work as he expected. He kept trying.

There were also a lot of other things for Faraday to do. The scientists at the Royal Institution were often employed by English businessmen to answer questions about products and equipment. Faraday spent months trying to find ways to make a stronger steel. He helped to investigate the cause of a fire in a sugar factory. He experimented with glass, working on lenses for telescopes.

Sally saw to it that his life was not spent entirely in the lab! If Michael could not find time to go outside the Royal Institution and visit friends and relatives, she invited them in. Two of their favorite guests were Constance and Jane, Sally's nieces. The girls loved to have Faraday bring something from his laboratory to show them. An unusual rock, bubbling chemicals, or a magnet would keep them interested for hours. Once Faraday brought a jar of worms called planaria. Sally retreated to the kitchen, but Constance and Jane were fascinated as Michael cut the worms into pieces and each piece grew into a complete worm. When he cut a head in two, two perfect heads developed.

Sometimes Constance and Jane brought their friends to the Royal Institution. If he had time, Faraday would put on a show for them in his laboratory. He might throw a soft, white powder called potassium into a bowl of water and watch with them as it exploded in a flash of light and a puff of smoke. Or he would let them watch as he sealed up some mercury in a bit of glass for them to take home.

Listening to the girls' questions, Michael remembered his own childhood. London must be full of children who were full of questions. Maybe the Royal Institution could do something to encourage that interest in science.

# 5
# Questions and Answers

"Think about how wonderful it is to live, to stand up and move about." Michael Faraday looked from the stage of the auditorium of the Royal Institution to the rows and rows of young faces in the audience. "Yet most people don't wonder about these things. They might think a mountain was wonderful, or a waterfall, but not the fact that they can walk around in the daytime and lie down at night."

It was Christmastime. Faraday had started a new tradition at the Royal Institution. Every year during the Christmas holidays, he gave lectures about science to the children who were on vacation from school. They might be tired of studying Latin or history, but they crowded into the auditorium to hear Faraday. Even the Prince of Wales, the future King of England, came to the Christmas lectures.

And Faraday liked giving the science talks. Standing on the stage, he remembered that first night when he had entered the same room to hear Sir Humphry Davy speak. Watching a girl write down the things he said, he remembered the 386 pages of notes he had taken from Davy's lectures. Seeing the puzzled frown on a boy's face, he recalled his own endless questions.

In the lectures he called "On The Various Forces of Matter," he talked about a power called gravity which pulls objects toward the earth and makes it possible for people to sit in chairs instead of flying around the room or floating off into space. He came out from behind the table and stood with one foot lifted. "Can you stand on one leg?" he asked.

"Yes," the children shouted.

"But it's a little awkward, isn't it? Do you see what I have to do when I stand on one leg like this? I move my body over the foot that's on the floor. That foot is called my *center of gravity* when I stand on it. Every object has a center of gravity, the place where the whole gravitating power of that object is centered. In order to stand up, you have to bring your body into a line over that center of gravity."

Faraday went on explaining how gravity works. He boiled water and balanced a bucket on a stick and described magic tricks that had mystified him as a boy. He knew that science was interesting only when the audience could see what he was talking about, so he acted out his lectures by doing all kinds of experiments that they could watch.

One year he gave six lectures called "The Chemical History of a Candle." He put an ordinary candle on his desk and asked it questions, just as he had always asked questions of everything. What makes a candle burn? Why is the flame always brighter toward the top? Where does the candle go when it has been burned down to a stump? Why does its light go out if you put it under a glass jar? Why do some candles smoke a great deal and others very little?

Usually, he told the children about some kind of experiment that they could do at home. After one of the lectures on candles, he told them to take a cold spoon and hold it over the flame of a candle. The spoon would then get a sort of mist over it. That showed that one of the products of a burning candle is water.

Sometimes Faraday had his desk piled with things the audience could take home and work with: bits of rock, pieces of wire, metals, or harmless chemicals. When he talked about static electricity, he told them how they could make a static electricity generator out of a piece of sealing wax, a watch, and a small wooden board.

The lectures were a change of pace from his long hours in the laboratory, and Faraday enjoyed them. But most of his time and energy were spent with his batteries and powders and jars and notebooks.

Visitors to his laboratory had to get used to some strong smells. One of Faraday's discoveries was a way to get the chemical benzene from fish oil. The room smelled of fish for weeks while he was working on that. Faraday was glad when he finished. Even though he was more or less used to the regular laboratory odors, the fish made him feel seasick after a few hours.

Once there was an explosion in a coal mine in the town of Haswell. No one knew what had caused the explosion, so Faraday was called in to decide the reason for the tragedy. There was a hearing at one of the buildings near the mine. Faraday sat at the front of the room and listened to the managers and miners tell what had happened on the day of the explosion. When they were through talking, he began to ask his questions.

"How do you measure the flow of air currents in the mine?" he asked first.

There was an inspector employed by the owners to check the air underground. He showed Faraday how he did this. He took a small box from his pocket and opened it.

"I just take a pinch of gunpowder, like this," he said, "and drop it on a candle flame." Someone lighted a candle, and the inspector tossed the gunpowder onto the flame. There was a

flash of light and a small "pop," and then a stream of black smoke rose from the candle. "In the mine," the inspector explained, "the smoke will go in the direction in which the air is moving. That is how I check the air currents."

Faraday nodded. He was thinking that the inspector was not very careful about explosives if he carried a box of gunpowder around in his pocket. This made Faraday think of another question.

"Where do you store your supply of gunpowder?" he asked.

"In a bag," the inspector said. "It's quite safe; we keep it tightly tied."

"And where do you keep the bag?"

"You're sitting on it!"

Faraday jumped up very quickly. The cushion on his chair was the powder bag—the softest thing the mine managers could find for the visiting expert to sit on!

Faraday decided that to prevent future explosions they would have to be more careful in storing and using gunpowder. He gave a large sum of money to the fund being collected for the families of the miners who had been killed.

In spite of all his projects and experiments, Michael found time to go to the theater. He would stand in line for tickets to anything from Punch and Judy shows to grand operas. But having grown up in London, he also could never get enough of the countryside and the outdoors. He exercised by taking walks: *long* walks. He and Sally's brother George thought nothing of taking a thirty-mile hike.

Michael read of a new invention: the velocipede. It was a machine that moved by means of human muscle-power; it was the ancestor of the modern bicycle. After studying a newspaper sketch of the contraption, he found some scraps of metal and wood and began building one. When it was finished, he brought Sally, George, Constance, and Jane to the wide hallway outside the lecture room of the Royal Institution. He climbed on the velocipede at the other end of the hall and rode it to them as the levers clacked and the wheels rattled. They all cheered, and then each one had a turn on the thing. The girls' legs were too short to make it go, but Faraday pushed them along and let them work the levers.

Afterwards, they all went back upstairs and played marbles on the floor using horse chestnuts.

The Faradays had no children of their own, so they liked to have Jane and Constance and their other nieces and nephews visit as often as possible. Michael usually kept some experiment going in the apartment to interest them.

Once he and the girls had twenty-three frogs laying eggs in a box in the corner. One morning they counted only twenty-one of the full-grown frogs. The next day there were nineteen. Where were the frogs going? At that point, Sally insisted that they take the frogs to a nearby park and let them go.

Constance caught a cold while staying with the Faradays, and Sally brought her to the laboratory early one morning to ask Michael to make her some cough drops. He put aside the experiment he was setting up and mixed an ugly purple paste in a pottery bowl. Rolling the stuff out on a piece of glass, he cut it into squares and let it dry.

The little girl made a face when she tasted the medicine, and Faraday smiled sympathetically. "I'll get you a bag of peppermints when your cold is better," he promised.

"What are you working on today?" Sally asked, wrapping Constance snugly in a warm shawl.

"Electricity. I'm hoping to find some way to make a steady current with a magnet."

"Ah, that again! Well, at least it doesn't smell as bad as the fish!"

## ...And More Questions

Faraday was not the only scientist trying to learn more about electricity. An Italian, Alessandro Volta, had been the one to discover how to make a simple battery. A battery produces small amounts of electricity from chemicals. Volta's battery used circles of zinc and copper separated by cloth soaked in salty water. A Frenchman, André Ampère, invented a device called a galvanometer which could measure electric power, much as electric meters today measure the amount of electricity used in a home or business.

And in 1825, a scientist named William Sturgeon made an electromagnet. He bent an iron bar into a horseshoe shape, wrapped it with copper wire, and sent an electric current through the wire. This turned the iron horseshoe into a powerful magnet that could hold as much as nine pounds of metal. As long as electric current went through the wire, the iron horseshoe was an electromagnet. When the current was turned off, it was just a piece of iron wrapped with wire.

Magnetism could be generated by electricity. Why couldn't electricity be generated by magnetism?

No one was able to do it. Wires were wrapped around magnets in every possible way, but the magnets did not make any electric current.

Faraday built a tiny model: an iron bar an inch long wrapped in a spiral of copper wire. He carried it in his vest pocket. When he was at a boring committee meeting or a long dinner party, he would take the model from his pocket and stare at it. What was the answer?

If people also stared at him and thought he was odd, Faraday did not worry about it.

He believed that everything in the world worked together in ways that made sense, if people could only understand. The energy or force of lightning, of sparks, of magnetism and electricity was the same energy in different forms. He was only trying to change the energy from one form to another.

One summer morning in 1831 Faraday sat on a high stool at his workbench in the laboratory, writing down the story of another failure. He had wrapped a large bar-shaped magnet with wire, but nothing had happened. It didn't seem to matter how powerful the magnet was; it would not make an electric current.

An officer of the Royal Institution came through the door,

carrying a large box. "Here, Faraday," he said, "you'll have to stop whatever you're doing and check these today."

"What?"

"Something for the Royal Navy."

The box contained samples of codfish. Some navy official wanted to know whether the dried fish was all right for the sailors to eat.

"Fish again!" Faraday grumbled to himself as he set up the equipment to analyze the stuff. Then he stopped and looked at the round lip of the glass beaker he was using. A circle! What if the magnet were round?

Later that day he had one of his helpers make a circle of soft iron. Faraday wrapped a coil of copper wire around one side of it. He called this Wire A. Around the other side of the ring he wrapped another wire, Wire B, which he attached to a galvanometer.

He then fastened Wire A to a small battery, sending an electrical charge through it which made the iron ring into an electromagnet. He hoped that this would cause a current to flow in the second wire, the one that was not connected to the battery.

The needle on the galvanometer moved, showing a charge in Wire B. It fell back immediately, but the needle moved again when Faraday disconnected Wire A from the battery.

Faraday stared at the galvanometer. Had it moved showing an electric current in Wire B—or was he imagining it? He connected the battery to Wire A again; the needle moved again. But the moment he pulled the Wire A connection away, the needle fell back. It moved when he moved Wire A.

The experiment seemed to show that electricity could be generated from magnetism. But Faraday was not satisfied. As usual, the answer he found only raised more questions. Why wasn't the current steady? Why did the electrical charge in Wire B show up only when he connected or disconnected the battery to Wire A? Why did the needle always swing back?

Faraday spent the next three weeks thinking about it. He wrote in a letter to a friend: "I am busy just now again on electromagnetism, and think I have got hold of a good thing, but can't say. It may be a weed instead of a fish that, after all my labour, I may at last pull up."

He repeated the experiment, using wires and magnets in many different shapes and sizes. He discovered that all he had to do was to move an electromagnet close to a coil of wire and the needle would jump.

The important thing was motion! It was a *moving* magnet that could generate electric power.

Faraday knew that if he placed a lot of tiny bits of iron on a sheet of white paper and then put a magnet under the paper, the bits of iron would arrange themselves in lines going out from the magnet. He believed that this meant there were "lines of force," like invisible muscles, that pulled metals toward the magnet. It was when something moved through these "lines of force" that an electric current was produced.

Next, he tried putting a disc or circle of copper between the ends of a large, horseshoe-shaped magnet, with wires attached to different points on the disc. When he turned the disc with a crank, the wires cut through the magnetic "lines of force" and a steady electrical charge showed on the meter.

Faraday had his answer.

Many years later, this idea was used by others to build a machine called a dynamo. It is the dynamo that generates the power to run our modern washing machines and television sets and electric ovens.

Faraday called the discovery that made the dynamo possible "magnetoelectric induction." It was fun to say. When Constance and Jane came to visit the laboratory, he showed them the experiment and told them its name. Then they could tell their friends: "Our uncle has discovered magnetoelectric induction."

"But what's the use of it?" people would ask Faraday when he told them about making electric current from magnetism.

He liked to quote the answer Benjamin Franklin had given when asked a similar question.

"What's the use of a baby?" Franklin had said. "Some day it will grow up!"

Faraday got very tired in the weeks and months when he was finding out about "magnetoelectric induction." He stayed in the laboratory for hours after everyone else had left and forgot to eat until Sally brought him a hot meal on a tray. One morning soon after the discovery he went to the laboratory and could not remember what he had been working on the night before.

Fresh air might help. Faraday put on his coat and went out through the tall doors at the front of the Royal Institution. The air was cold and damp, but it did make Faraday feel better after he had walked a few blocks. He would have to take a vacation. He and Sally could go to some quiet beach miles from London, and he would let his mind rest for a few weeks. Then he would be ready to go back to the laboratory.

Two young boys, walking toward Michael, were staring at him and whispering to each other. Finally one of them said shyly, "Good morning, Mr. Faraday."

Michael smiled and said, "Good morning. May I ask how you gentlemen know my name?"

"We went to your Christmas lectures, sir," said the boy who had spoken before.

"*All* of them." The second boy grinned and shifted a stack of school books from one arm to the other.

"That's fine. . . ." Faraday waved to them and walked on. He watched the traffic in the street— fine carriages, grocery carts, soldiers on horseback, tall wagons—and remembered how he had dodged through those same streets with his newspapers when he had been Mr. Riebau's errand boy.

He had just come to the end of the block when the same two boys came dashing around the corner, pink-cheeked and puffing.

"Good morning, Mr. Faraday," they said again.

"Well, you two look familiar. Haven't I seen you somewhere before?"

They giggled. "We wondered if you'd tell us what the Christmas lectures will be about this year, sir," the tallest one said.

"I haven't decided yet," Faraday told them. "Perhaps they may have something to do with electricity."

"Oh, that would be first-rate!" said the second boy.

Michael reached into his vest pocket, thinking that he might have some of the peppermints he kept for Constance and Jane. He felt the model he had used when he was trying to imagine how to make electric current from magnetism.

"Here," he said, holding it out to them. "I'm through with this now, but it might give you something to think about."

They thanked him and raced off, beaming. "Ask questions," he called after them. "Never stop asking questions!"

# Author's Note

Michael Faraday lived and worked for many years after his great discovery that made the dynamo possible. From his laboratory in the Royal Institution came other ideas that are still being used today.

He discovered a process called "electrolysis" which made it possible to plate metals to each other. Electrolysis is used to make gold-plated jewelry, chromium-plated bumpers for automobiles, and a new kind of printing called "electrotype."

He learned how to turn many gases into liquids. His discovery was the basis for the liquid gases used more than a hundred years later as rocket fuel.

He had the idea that light moves through space in waves or lines, like the "lines of force" of magnetism. People thought this was a very strange theory. Nobody could see any lines in the sky! But scientists today agree that Faraday was right.

Michael Faraday's questioning came to an end a few months after he gave his last Christmas lectures. He died on August 25, 1867. But he had started something that did not stop when he died. Many years later, his dynamo generated the power to run all kinds of inventions that no one dreamed of in his day. And all over England, boys and girls who had heard his lectures fiddled with wire and string and rocks and anything else they could find, making up their own experiments—and, of course, always asking questions.

# Glossary

**BATTERY**  An instrument that uses chemicals to generate electricity.

**CURRENT**  A flow of electricity.

**DYNAMO**  A machine that uses magnetism to generate electric power.

**ELECTROMAGNET**  A magnet made by wrapping a wire around a piece of soft iron and sending electricity through the wire.

**EXPERIMENT**  A test used by scientists to find out something or to learn how and why something works.

**LABORATORY**  A room or building where experiments are done.

**LECTURE**  A speech in which the speaker tries to teach something to the listeners.

**MAGNET**  An object that attracts iron and other substances.

**MAGNETOELECTRIC INDUCTION**  Faraday's name for the process he discovered for generating electricity from magnetism. The process today is usually called "electromagnetic induction."

**MERCURY**  A liquid metal.

**METER**  An instrument used to measure electric current.

**STATIC ELECTRICITY**  An electric charge that, when produced, stays in one place, unlike current electricity which flows.

# Bibliography

Agassi, Joseph. *Faraday as a Natural Philosopher*. Chicago: University of Chicago Press, 1971.

Burton, Elizabeth. *The Pageant of Georgian England*. New York: Scribner's, 1967.

Faraday, Michael. *The Chemical History of a Candle*. New York: Thomas Y. Crowell Co., 1957.

————. *On the Various Forces of Nature*. New York: Thomas Y. Crowell Co., 1957.

Ginzburg, Benjamin. *The Adventure of Science*. New York: Tudor, 1932.

Harvey, Tad. *The Quest of Michael Faraday*. Garden City, New York: Garden City Books, 1961.

Kendall, James. *Young Chemists and Great Discoveries*. Freeport, N.Y.: Books for Libraries Press, 1969.

May, Charles Paul. *Michael Faraday and the Electric Dynamo*. New York: Franklin Watts, 1961.

Perry, George. *The Victorians: A World Built to Last*. New York: Viking Press, 1974.

Quinlan, Maurice. *Victorian Prelude*. Hamden, Conn.: Archon Books, 1965.

Randell, Wilfrid L. *Michael Faraday*. Boston: Small, Maynard Co., 1924.

Williams, L. Pearce. *Michael Faraday*. New York: Basic Books, 1965.

## About the Author

Nancy Veglahn is a graduate teaching assistant and a teacher of freshman composition at South Dakota State University. She received her BA from Morningside College in Sioux City, Iowa, and is now planning to study for a master's degree.

Carrying on a family tradition—her mother is also a writer—Mrs. Veglahn is the author of numerous children's books, such as *The Vandals of Treason House*, *Swimmers Take Your Marks*, and *Buffalo King: The Story of Scotty Phillip*.

The author lives in Brookings, South Dakota, with her husband, Don, and their two children, Dan and Ruth.

## About the Artist

Christopher Spollen is a graduate of the High School of Art and Design and the Parsons School of Design in New York City.

His original etchings are reproduced here, as well as in *Tales from the Steppes* and *Mishka, Pishka and Fishka*. One of Mr. Spollen's etchings for *Tales from the Steppes* won the distinction of being in the Society of Illustrators' show in New York City.

Mr. Spollen is a free-lance illustrator and lives on Staten Island, New York.